This book is dedicated to Stirling and all the horses, past and present, of the Household Cavalry.

STIRLING 7447

My Life Story

Written by Alan Scrymgeour

ASP EQUINE

www.asp-equine.com

STIRLING 7447: MY LIFE STORY

by Alan Scrymgeour

Cover photography by Alan Scrymgeour

Story written by Alan Scrymgeour

Book design by Alan Scrymgeour

ASP-EQUINE is a subsidiary of Alan Scrymgeour Photography.

www.asp-equine.com

alan@asp-equine.com

07432708105

CONTENTS

INTRODUCTION - p7

Chapter 1. BORN TO THE CAVALRY - p9

Chapter 2. TRAINING THE INSTRUCTORS - p17

Chapter 3. NO ORDINARY RANK AND FILE - p37

Chapter 4. NORTHERN IRELAND - p47

Chapter 5. BACK IN THE TROOPS - p55

Chapter 6. A STRIDE TOO FAR - p69

Chapter 7. MY FOREVER HOME - p79

STIRLING, MY FRIEND by Lorraine Olsen - p91

ACKNOWLEDGEMENTS - p93

Introduction

MY LIFE STORY

As the sun breaks through the morning mist and slowly warms my tired old bones, I feel the years of parade ground drills weighing heavy on my back. From the sanctuary of my field overlooking Windsor, I watch as the royal standard is hoisted atop the Castle on the horizon. The Queen is in residence. I find myself standing to attention, as I always did on parade and the memories come flooding back. My name is Stirling 7447, retired horse of the Household Cavalry – Queen's Life Guard and this is my Life story.

Chapter 1

BORN INTO THE CAVALRY

My story starts far from Windsor, where I live now, in Kecskemét, Hungary, on the yard of the then World Carriage Driving Champion, Laslo Yuash. A visiting friend and fellow competitor, Cavalry Officer Lieutenant Colonel Hywell Davis, was looking for a new team of horses to compete in the forthcoming World Championships.

Hungarian carriage horses are world renowned for their speed, strength and stamina which makes them ideal for competitive carriage driving. My father, Marka, was one of the Hungarian warmblood/Nonius stallions that Laslo and Hywell painstakingly put together for the task.

Lt Colonel Davis was stationed in Germany with the Armoured Division of the Household Cavalry. In 1986 the newly formed Stallion Team were shipped to Germany where Hywell Davis began to train the young horses into a tight world class team.

My father, Marka, was a fine upper-class stallion with good breeding and a strong personality. He stood sixteen and a half hands at the shoulder and when paired with Legeny was a formidable driving team. In harness he really knew his job, strong, agile and intelligent. Off the course, he had a special skill for escaping from his stable, which would be of importance later in my life story.

The bond between Marka and his Groom Patricia Preston was a strong one, but on the odd occasion his excitement and strength would result in a few exuberant accidents. Marka loved to be brushed by his Groom, standing motionless in his stall for her to make him shine like a Cavalry Guards helmet badge. Only a sweet polo treat went down better.

The Stallion team under the reins of Lt Colonel Davis became a very successful team in competition. With the Colonels' skill at precision driving, and Marka and Legeny schooled to perfection, all the hard work and effort resulted in a very respectable twentieth place at the 1988 World Championships in Ascot.

In January 1988 Lt Colonel Davis gave up his command in Germany and relocated to Windsor. The Stallion team followed on shortly after. Finding a suitable barrack for the team was difficult, but finally they were re-homed in the coaching stables at Windsor Barracks adjacent to the Household Cavalry stable blocks.

I never met my father, but his strong Hungarian spirit flows through my veins and I am proud to call him my father.

In contrast to my father's Eastern European roots, my mother was born and bred on the lush green fields of County Donegal in Ireland. Like many Irish Draft horses before her, she was acquired by the Army at the Donegal horse sales and shipped over to England to join the ranks of the Household Cavalry.

When my mother arrived at the Defence Animal Centre in Melton Mowbray for assessment, it must have been a real shock for her. One minute, grazing on a rainy, wind-swept field in rural Ireland, the next minute being unloaded, frightened and confused from a windowless horse transporter into the blinding light of a very alien environment.

After an initial assessment and a move to the Cavalry Training Barracks in Windsor, my mother - number 7024, began training under the tutorage of the Cavalry riding staff. It was noted by an instructor, Corporal of Horse Richard Maxwell, that 7024 had a natural raw talent for dressage which marked her out from the herd.

Richard Maxwell was a very accomplished dressage rider. As my mother underwent her initial training, Richard began to build a strong horse and rider bond between them. My mother, small and light on her feet, showed great promise as a dressage horse with great aptitude for the discipline needed to compete at the highest level. In time, Richard and my mother became a formidable team on the national dressage circuit. Whilst competing at a series of dressage events, a star of the show jumping world approached the Army to buy my mother for their stable. The offer would have seen my mother re-homed to a prestigious yard and given the luxury a top-flight horse deserves, but the offer was rejected by the Army and she carried on competing with Richard to great success.

In 1985, after finishing her riding training, my mother was officially inducted into the ranks of the Household Cavalry Mounted Division. As tradition dictates it wasn't until this point that my mother, Cavalry horse number 7024 was given her name. Each consecutive year is allocated a letter of the alphabet and all Cavalry horses inducted in that year are given names beginning with the allocated letter. In 1988 all new inductees were given a name beginning in the letter 'M' and she was given the name Moonstone.

Moonstone began her military career in the ranks of 3 Troop - The Life Guard Squadron. She was stationed at the Household Cavalry barracks in Knightsbridge, London and became a well-liked and integral part of her troop.

In the history of the Household Cavalry there has only been four horses born into the Cavalry. I am one of those special horses.

In January 1988, Marka and his fellow team of driving horses were stabled in the coach horse stable in Windsor, adjacent to the Cavalry regiments stable block. One night, under unknown circumstances, Marka slipped his tether and proceeded to wander the lines of stable blocks at his will. At the same time Moonstone, quietly resting in her stall, was oblivious to the master escapologist on the loose.

As the guard made its regular rounds they came upon Marka wandering the walkway of Moonstones stable block. Horrified at the sight of a strange horse wandering around the troop, the guard attempted to capture Marka and return him to his stable. It took two guards to finally capture and remove Marka from the stable block and march him back to his unlocked chain. It wasn't the first time Marka or one of the other stallions had escaped their stable. A report was made to the officers in the morning but there was no cause to be alarmed at the ever more frequent adventure.

It wasn't until eleven months later when Moonstone and Richard Maxwell were at an event that something strange was noticed. Richard and Moonstone were attending a local Pony Club to hold a military style boot camp for the club. As Richard readied Moonstone for the day, he noticed that when he fastened her saddle girth strap Moonstone started to lactate. It must have been quite a shock for Richard, but I think my mother knew what was going on. Once Moonstone was returned to barracks, Richard explained to the Veterinary Staff about his findings. A scan was ordered for Moonstone and right enough she was found to be with foal - me. The Veterinary Staff were able to tell how old I was at that point by measuring my eye socket to estimate my due date. After the pregnancy and delivery date was assessed, Moonstone was transported to the Defence Animal Centre at Melton Mowbray for the imminent birth.

In total there was three foals attributed to Lt Colonel Davis's stallions over the period of their stay. The clue to their guilt is in the description, 'stallions'. When a young male remount is brought over from Ireland they are gelded, so the evidence led to Hywell's team. A letter from Andrew Parker-Bowles, the Commanding Officer of the Household Cavalry was promptly delivered to Lt Colonel Davis asking him to either remove them from the stables or he'll turn them loose on the M4. Hywell acted upon those very precise orders and re-homed the whole team in a more secure stable on the outskirts of Windsor.

On the 2 December 1988 I was born in the veterinary wing of the Defence Animal Centre at Melton Mowbray. Like my mother's delivery by transporter from Ireland some eleven years earlier, my delivery at the same stable block was an equally traumatic experience.

My arrival was met with amazement from the small gathering of staff who crowded at the stable door to watch. Lying in the straw, cold, wet and semi-blind, I felt an overwhelming urge to get up onto my legs. Finding my feet proved difficult at first, but as I would prove throughout my life I had a determination that would never give up. I will never forget those first few weeks bonding with my mother on the green pastures of Melton Mowbray. From the moment I was born, I showed a strong spirit and a feisty temperament, thanks to the mix of Irish draft and Hungarian thoroughbred in me.

At the time of my birth my mother, Moonstone, was eleven years old and in the prime of her life. After a short time away from her troop nurturing me, my mother and I were moved to the Cavalry Regiment barracks in Windsor. Gradually my mother was integrated back into her troop duties and I was entrusted to the Farrier Major for supervision. I will always remember Farrier Major Carl Jones – A massive man with a fearsome look and hands that could bend iron without using his hammer.

While my mother took her place in the Queens Life Guard parades, I would be led along by the Farrier Major trying to keep time with the marching ranks. I think it must have been quite a sight; The Farrier Major, tall, smart and proud, marching in time – me all excited and bouncing to my own beat. My mother was a small horse compared to most of her fellow Cavalry horses, but dressed in her Ceremonial kit she looked over ten feet tall. As I grew up I was inpatient to take my place on the parade ground.

Chapter 2

TRAINING THE INSTRUCTORS

Early one morning, instead of following my mother out of our stable block, as I had done many times before, I was taken on my own to a new area in the barracks that I had never seen before. My groom led me across a concrete paddock towards a large building with a high roof. Standing in the middle of the room were two lone figures, both wearing riding instructor outfits. As we approached the men in the middle of the room, one of the instructors stepped forward. My groom, saluted, then announced that my number was 7447. 7447. 7447. The room was so large that the numbers echoed around the room as if to emphasise the significance of the number. That was the first time I heard my Household Cavalry Number and it would stay with me forever.

Stabled with my mother at the Windsor Barracks, I had led a charmed life shadowing her as she went about her duties. When my mother was not on parade we would be together being fussed over by all manner of visitors. But that meeting with these two uniformed gentlemen had a different air about it. There seemed to be a seriousness but calming air to them. The solider who had stepped forward at that first meeting was Corporal of Horse Joe Weller – a senior riding instructor. I was three and a half years old and this was the start of my training, which would see me be inducted into the Household Cavalry in my mother's footsteps.

The Household Cavalry Riding Staff were a team of twelve men affectionately known as the 'Blue Mafia'. Every year the Riding Staff were tasked with training the remounts (new horses) for the Cavalry. As Joe started to walk me around the in-door riding school, he noted that I had a very different temperament from the usual Irish draft horse he was used to working with. It wasn't until he clipped on a long lunge rein and watched me move around him, in ever quickening circles, that he first saw my secret weapon.

The Household Cavalry was created in the 17th century to be King Charles II private body guard. King Charles decreed that all Cavalry horses must be black in colour; he thought that black horses struck fear into the hearts of the enemy. In my prime, I had a different way of striking fear in people.

From as early as I can remember, I always felt an urge to run. An uncontrollable urge to run fast and forever. I don't know where it came from, but it has always bubbled under my skin, like an itch that I could never scratch enough. So, when Joe gave me permission to show my hidden talents, I let him have it. Progression from a semi-controlled walk to full on flaming haired banshee was instantaneous.

At the end of that first assessment with the riding staff, I never went back to my mothers' side again. Instead of being stabled in the main Cavalry stables next to my mother, I was walked over to the training wing of the barracks. My new stable was another brick-built building which looked almost identical to my last. As I was led to my allocated stable box, past stall after stall of young horses, there was no sign of my mum.

From the outside, the new stable block had a cold looking exterior, but inside it was a hive of activity. Inside the block was the same orange iron pillars and beams that I saw in my old stables, the same smell of straw filling the air, the same green overalled men going about their business. It all seemed familiar but new.

I strode down the central aisle, head up and taking in all the newness of the surroundings. I glanced at each nervous looking horse as I past them by. Each horse was wearing a head collar and tethered to the wall, nervously shuffling in their new surroundings, with newly clipped coats, hogged manes and plucked tails.
As we reached an empty stall in the line of occupied

boxes, the groom led me in to the small space. On both sides of the stall were six foot high wooden screens and a solid red brick wall at the end. He made me face the wall before tying my lead rope onto a silver ring. I looked up and saw a small slit of a window tantalisingly just out of reach above me. A blinking fluorescent tube hung above me which illuminated my bleak, anonymous box just big enough for me and my groom. I was not sure I liked this new place.

Standing alone in my box, my ears back and my eyes wide open, I started to throw my head in annoyance at my new surroundings. Suddenly from behind me I felt a firm warm hand on my rump which slowly moved along my body until it finally touched my neck, when it started to gently scratch me. 'Oh, that felt good'. I felt the same calming hand placed under my chin and a softly reassuring voice telling me, "Everything will be alright, don't worry, we'll look after you". It was the hand and voice of the Corporal of Horse who was very much in charge of the stable block. That kind voice, was a voice I heard a lot in those first few years of training, mostly at full volume and mostly shouting at the young troopers. Despite his fearsome bark he always kept his word.

At 06:00 each morning the young troopers would assemble for their morning duties. With yellow headed brushes in hand the first chore of the morning was mucking out. The corners of each box were heaped up with straw, like a straw drift. I loved to flick it around with my feet at night when I was bored. In the morning as the fluorescent lights blinked into life it looked like a blizzard of straw had blown through the block.

Training was a daily occurrence. Once I had shown that I could control my urge to run at a million miles per hour, the next step was to put a saddle and rider on my back. At first, I didn't like the feeling of the saddle on my back. But as Joe held my reins, softly reassuring me, I allowed another instructor to bear his weight on me, then hoist himself onto the saddle. I wasn't sure at first. I hadn't experienced anything like this before. But Joe kept softly reassuring me, I trusted Joe, so I allowed the rider to stay on my back. After a short while Joe let go of the lunge rope and it was just me and my rider. It was an unusual feeling to feel the motion of the rider on my back; moving in rhythm with me. His knees gripping me tightly; his legs gently brushing my side; the feeling in my mouth as the rider gently guided me around the arena. I felt strangely responsible for the rider on my back.

Some days my training didn't go quite so well. Depending on how I felt that day, sometimes I could be a real challenge to control. Because I was so challenging, only the riding staff were allowed to ride me. Some days I even gave the riding staff, who were all excellent horsemen, a real run for their money. I seemed to have the devil in me. I was never nasty, I never wanted to hurt anyone, I just wanted to run, to feel free from all the standing around in my 6 x 10 box. Some of the other horses would bite and kick anyone who came near them but not me. I just wanted to run, to run fast, to be mischievous, to do things in my own way.

I was always a small horse. I seemed to stop growing about five and a half years old. How I could tell, was, it never got any easier to look over the wooden partitions of my stall to see what everyone else was doing. If I could have stood on a young trooper's back to see better, I would have.

It took me quite a while to settle into the role of a Cavalry remount. Other less flighty horses came and went before I had reached a sufficient level to advance in my training. However, once Joe Weller judged me proficient with walking, trotting and cantering, with a rider on my back, I was ready for the next challenge – Ceremonial Training.

Before I could begin my ceremonial training, I needed to be picked to join a specific Squadron of the Household Cavalry. This was a big deal. This selection would see me join a new family for my whole career. My mother was a Life Guard horse and when she died in 1999 she had been in the ranks for over twenty years.
On the day of the Squadron selection I was washed, cleaned, scrubbed and polished. They gave me a smart soldiers shave and partly bandaged my tail. As we paraded

in the in-door school in front of the panel of uniformed officers, my groom wore a bib with a number on it. As the officers from both Squadrons watched, we horses walked in a line and they made their choices. I walked with my usual exuberance and style. Walking back and forth, I tried to look impressive. If the officer was looking for a guard horse who was strong and fast then I was his 'man'. As the numbers on the groom's bibs were read out we were lined up in separate lines. I found myself in the Life Guards – Just like my mother.

Despite passing my initial riding training, I was still quite a difficult horse to control. I had my own way of doing things. In those early days, I had a massive attitude. In my head I was a big 18 hands Olympic Gold winning super horse. I could be rideable one day then uncontrollable the next, depending on my mood. I have always been my own 'person'.

After eighteen months on the training wing at Windsor barracks, I was loaded onto a transporter and taken to Knightsbridge in London. On arrival at the Hyde Park Barracks, the home of the Household Cavalry, I was unloaded from the lorry and tentatively eased my way down the lorries ramp. As I found my footing on the concrete yard, I looked around my new surroundings and tried to take it all in. Beyond the small concrete courtyard was a four-storey red brick building with a large round royal crest on it. As I stood, all excited and eager to see why I was there, I noticed a loud noise coming from the direction of the main gate. While training in Windsor we had been taken out of the barracks and ridden on the local roads, with cars and lorries respectfully driving around us. The noise coming from beyond the walls in all directions was similar but much louder.

I reluctantly followed a trooper who had taken my rein. He led me inside to an altogether quieter sound scape. The Knightsbridge stables didn't look much different from the one's I just left in Windsor. The same size 10 x 6 stall, the same heaped corners of straw, the same urgency in the trooper's activity and the same lovely forage to eat.

I love food. I always have. In the Cavalry, you're always really well looked after. You get the best of everything, and that goes for the food as well. Because of my constant activity, even when in my box, I burn off my food really quickly. So, when it comes to food I can never get enough.

What do I mean by 'Constant Activity'? Well, I mean I was constantly on the move, trying to do things in my box. Sometimes, I would try to kick the straw into the aisle at troopers walking by. Other times, I would try to undo my rope from the ring on the wall, so I could go for a wander. Other times, I would try to nip the troopers as they brushed my back. I just wanted to be doing something. I always had a zest for life. I always wanted to make the best of what I had. That didn't always mean I was sweetness and light. I could be real trouble.

My Cavalry training resumed at Knightsbridge with Lance Corporal Fraser MacDonald teaching me how to be a model Guard Horse. Fraser, was a really good rider, I could feel that he really knew how to ride. His balance, his subtle controls with his hands, his confidence with me made me feel relaxed. Sometimes my training would go well, but other times I wouldn't feel like doing what he wanted to do. I just wanted to run and have fun. Even when Fraser started training me to wear the ceremonial kit, which was so heavy, I would cheekily try to shake it off my back, or throw my head to loosen my bridle. Fraser was very patient with me and I think secretly enjoyed my good meaning fun and games.

I always did things at speed. I had a really fast walk. If I was asked to, "trot-on", by my rider, he would have to ride me on a really short rein; I would go from manageable to lunatic in a blink of an eye. The tighter the rein, the better the chance the rider had of controlling me. I was quite responsive to my rider's commands, and I would stop when I was asked, but the urge to go fast was so strong in me that I couldn't resist the chance to let it all go.

When I was fitted with my 'Black Kit', the leather straps and buckles of my ceremonial kit, I was fitted with an extra adaptation to my tack. It was called a Martingale. The idea of giving me a Martingale was to stop me lifting or carrying my head too high when I was being ridden.

Over the years, I have surprised a lot of riders with the action of my head. When I start to move forward my head and neck always lifts up very high. It's something I can't control, when I'm walking, that's not a problem. When I go from a walk to a trot or canter, the rider gets such a fright. As their body weight moves forward to counteract the forward movement, my head rears right up, right in their face. It all happens so quickly, that if the rider is not careful, they can bash their faces on the back of my head. I don't mean to hurt them, but you have to be on your game when you ride me. So that's why I have a Martingale on my 'Black Kit'.

The Martingale is only a few bits of leather and brass. When you add this to the already substantial weight of the ceremonial kit, it makes no difference. When I was dressed in my full ceremonial kit, with Fraser dressed in his mounted review order, I had an extra eighteen stone to carry on my small frame. It was hard, but didn't Fraser and I look amazing? Fraser, in his scarlet tunic with sleek white plume and shiny jack boots. Me, with my dazzling Black kit, shiny hoofs and a twinkle in my eye. We looked the business, real dapper. Moonstone would have been proud of me.

My mother was stationed at the same Knightsbridge barracks as I was. When I started my training in Windsor she was taken back to her original troop to resumed her Life Guard duties. Moonstone was a 3 Troop horse. I would see her from time to time on the parade ground or as she walked past my stable box, but we didn't get much time together.

As one lady slowly drifted from my thoughts another would enter my life. The first time I met Debbie MacDonald was when Fraser prepared me early one morning for a special event. I could hear lots of voices coming from the in-door school across the courtyard. As Fraser jumped on my back, we headed over to the school. I started to get excited at meeting the waiting crowd. As we reached the door of the school, I decided to make a grand entrance for the assembled crowd. As Fraser lined me up with the open door, I took off. As we entered the large room, everyone's gaze was on me. I had already reached cantering speed, but I was sideways. As Fraser and I reached the middle room, I came to an abrupt stop. I'm sure the onlookers could hear a, "Ta-Dah!" from me, as I announced that I had arrived. The crowd just stood in amazement. Now that's what I call an entrance.
In 1996 the Household Cavalry decided to try an experiment. Due to the low level of manpower in the Cavalry at this time, the top brass decided to employ civilian grooms and riders to help the troopers with the work load. The crowd of men and women, who gathered

It wasn't all fun and games in the Regiment. There were serious occasions which demanded me to try and be serious. Like the first time Fraser took me on a Queen's Escort parade. The day started with a good wash down in the yard and a groom to make me shine like a new penny. The kit was next. Having the ceremonial kit put on me was a slow business. With every piece of kit strapped on, you could feel the weight of history in each leather strap and silver buckle. My bridle alone had eleven separate straps and twenty-five buckles. When it was fitted correctly, I felt every one. Placed under my saddle was a sheepskin rug which added more weight but most of all it acted like a radiator making me sweat even on the coldest of days. The weight was almost unbearable.

As I was tacked up with my ceremonial kit, a tug on my girth strap, an adjustment of my bridle and I was ready for the parade. Inside the barracks, Fraser was also being dressed up with his ceremonial kit. As he emerged from the barracks, slipping and sliding his way down the ramp into the courtyard, I stood waiting for him by the white washed mounting block. The way he walked towards me in his highly polished Jack boots made me giggle. He looked like a robot, walking as stiff legged as possible, trying not to crease the hard-earned mirror shine on his impressive boots. Once Fraser was in the saddle we were ready for the inspection.
The courtyard was a buzz with horses, guards and officers, all readying themselves for something. The place

was electric with excitement and industry. I could feel that something special was about to happen. I had no idea how 'special' it was going to be.

A line of guards and their horses started to form facing the barracks. We were 130 horses strong and ready to be inspected by the officers. If we passed their very particular inspection, we could take part in the days event. When a Life Guard and his mount are inspected there are fifty or more different elements which must be correctly fitted and cleaned.

As the line of horses and guards squared up, I took my place. Fraser lined me up with the horses on either side. I looked along the line of black horses as they nodded, shuffled and stamped in anticipation. I really had no idea what was going on but my excitement was reaching fever pitch. Fraser could feel me beneath him, my blood starting to pump, almost bouncing on the spot with expectancy. Like a father, knowingly reassuring his child to keep calm and relax, Fraser clapped me and whispered in my ear, which made me take a deep breath and calm down.

With a loud, "Guard, Attention!", the riders stiffened in their saddles. The Inspecting Officer stepped forward. Starting at the furthest end of the line he slowly inspected every detail of each horse and guard. When he reached Fraser and myself I felt the officers gaze looking in minute in the in-door school that day, was the first intake of grooms and riders waiting to take their proficiency tests. Among the crowd was a wonderful young lady called Debbie. At a later date she would become my rider Fraser's wife. I think I had a lot to do with Fraser catching Debbie's eye by making him look like a riding God, as he tamed my unforgettable entrance that morning.

The civilian riders and grooms helped swell the ranks of the troopers and made exercising and looking after us horses more manageable. Fraser was my sole rider at this time, due to my antics, but Debbie was such a good rider that she was granted permission to ride me out. When Fraser was away or busy training other remounts, Debbie would take me around Hyde Park for exercise. I loved to be in the park, running around the all-weather ridding track at Mach One with the wind rushing through my mane and scaring the wildlife. Debbie and I would watch all the goings on in the park and enjoy the changing seasons cast new colours over the trees.

Every morning Debbie would walk into my stable block and call my name. As she walked along the lines of horses waking from their slumber, I would pop my head up as high as I could over the partition of my stall and look for her coming along the aisle. As Debbie reached my stall and said, "Good morning", I would pull faces at her to make her laugh.

detail at how I was turned out. Starting at my head, he scrutinised my nose band, then my brow band and on around me until he appeared back in front of me again. Next, he moved his gaze up to Fraser, eyeing up his cuirass, his helmet, his plume and so on. The way the rider carries himself in the saddle, also matters to the officer's inspection. I felt Fraser pull himself up as upright and straight as he could, so I did the same. I stood as tall and proud looking as I could, so Fraser looked his best.

Once the inspecting officer was satisfied that all horses and Guards looked at their best the order was given to file out of front gate to begin the walk to Buckingham Palace. In pairs, we formed a long snaking line, walking nose to tail, which stopped the traffic. The public stopped and watch us pass them by. Mums knelt down and pointed us out to their toddlers in their push chairs. Dads with kids on their shoulders stopped and explained who we were. Tourists stopped their sightseeing and pointed. I heard a multitude of foreign languages all excitedly talking amongst their groups as we reached Buckingham Palace, where we rendezvoused with The Queen's State Carriage.

In the inner courtyard of Buckingham Palace the Queens State Carriage was waiting for the Queen to take her seat on board. Fraser and myself stood on our 'mark' outside the courtyard, ready to receive the Queen. As the Escort Commander saluted, that was our signal that the Queen was seated and on her way. As the State Carriage emerged from the Palace courtyard, I couldn't believe my eyes; what an amazing sight. Six stunning white horses pulling a dazzling gold stage coach with outriders and a line of Cavalry Officers escorting the carriage to the rear. As the carriage passed me by, Fraser turned us to join the lengthening line of Life Guards escorting the Carriage.

Following the Queen's carriage down The Mall, trotting towards Wellington Arch, was an experience that I will never forget. Crowds of people lined the barriers, cheering and waving, I was so proud to be part of such an amazing spectacle. Fraser had to keep me calm. A couple of times my excitement of the occasion got the better of me but Fraser was up to the challenge and soon calmed me down. I tried to take in all the sights as the line of horses and guards bounced in unison, with their plumes swaying and the sound of our horse shoes on the tarmac. All too soon, we arrived at Westminster and the Houses of Parliament. While the Queen performed her time-honoured duty of opening parliament, Fraser and I stood outside awaiting the return duty.

This was the first time I had been involved in a State occasion. I participated in many state parades but that first time was always a special memory. Once I had a couple of escort duties under my belt, I was adjudged to be ready to be passed out as an official Life Guard Horse. Up to this point I was referred to as, '7447'. When a horse is officially inducted into the Regiment they receive a name and squadron number. I was passed out in front of Commanding Officer Colonel Massey and became part of the rich history of the Household Cavalry Mounted Division.

When a horse is passed out to a troop, he is given a unique squadron number. My number is LG24, LG stands for Life Guards. All Household Cavalry horses have their squadron number branded onto their legs in a very specific way. My right front leg has LG on it, my left has 24 branded on it and I have a microchip in me.
The most important identification a horse gets when it's 'passed out', is its name. Major Robertson was given the honour of naming my years intake of horses. The Household Cavalry have a simple system for naming a year's group of horses. It uses the same first letter, in the sequence of the alphabet, just like a car has a registration with a year prefix. My years letter was 'S'. The alphabetical system of naming horses gives a riding trooper an indication of when the horse was inducted into the Troop, and that would tell him how experienced that horse was at doing his duties. If the present year was a 'U' registration then he knew that the 'S' Reg horse he was about to ride was not an experienced mount and he had to be very cautious on duty with it.

Major Robertson, a fine Scottish gentleman, gave me the distinguished name of STIRLING. I was named after the battle of Stirling. He didn't particularly know me but maybe someone had explained to him that some days you had to battle me in the saddle. My official name, number and squadron number from that day on was - Stirling 7447 LG24.

The more I wore the Ceremonial kit on my duties, the more I developed a bad back. Fraser noticed that I was struggling to take the weight of my kit and he decided to take me off my ceremonial duties to let my back recover. I was assigned light duties and given time to recover from the strain. It was a relief not to have to carry the kit at least twice a week, instead, I was allowed to recuperate hacking out with Fraser and Debbie in less weighty civilian tack.

If a horse proves to be a difficult horse, or becomes sick or ill, then they are moved to what Fraser called 'The Sick Lines'. I was stabled in the sick lines while my back got stronger. Debbie MacDonald helped to get me fit again, slowly rehabilitating me until I didn't show any signs of pain. While Fraser didn't ride me in any ceremonial duties, because of my back, he did start to ride me in local show jumping competitions. As an instructor, Fraser was expected to fly the flag for the Household Cavalry at numerous equestrian competitions in and around Windsor. My mother, Moonstone, was competing with Richard Maxwell at top class dressage events for the same reason. Fraser took me on the show jumping circuit for six months to build up my strength. I proved to be a fearless competitor. I would take on any obstacle in front of me and at great speed, sometimes not a great combination.

To be a good show jumper you need to be sensitive to the commands of your rider, where as I could be a bit too flighty and excitable to be a serious show jumper. Myself and Fraser had much more success competing in the tent pegging arena. Together we were very good at this discipline. Tent pegging calls for the horse to be fast and straight, something I could do better than most horses. We won a whole host of competitions together. One such competition was the championships held at Amber Court. We were pitted against fellow Army horses, Police horses and other local competitors. We beat them all, winning the championships for the Household Cavalry. Once I had recovered from my back injury, I was moved back into 3 Troop's stable. I was not very happy at being back in the troops again. Going back to the duties of a Life Guard horse made me very grumpy. I took my unhappiness out on my mother. The mother and son bond between us was never that strong, probably because of the lack of time we had together when I was first born. When we were together Moonstone and I used to fight. The decision was taken to move me to another troop – 1 Troop. A new troop meant another stable block, but the same old routine.

Chapter 3

NO ORDINARY RANK AND FILE

With my move to a new troop came the opportunity to meet new people. Moving from my mother's troop was a sad occasion, but I have always looked on the bright side of life and tried to make the best of what I was dealt. As my mother was taken out of my life again, another lady took her place. Jo Darlington was a civilian groom allocated to work with 1 troop. Each Life Guard troop had a civilian groom and civilian rider allocated to help with the up keep and exercising of the horses. Although Jo was employed to look after all the troops horses, I think she took special care of me. Jo really loved me, her mother even cross stitched a picture of Jo and myself for her wall.

Fraser had trained me so well that I could be ridden by other riders without me losing my cool. Jo was allowed to help exercise me when she could. Jo and I had some fun. I would play games with her in the park. Well, I mean, I would play a game with her on me. Jo always exercised me around the riding track in Hyde Park. The thin strip of soft dirt that wound its way around the outside of Hyde Park for a few miles. As we hacked in the fresh air I would hatch a plan for the day's entertainment. For instance, when we would get to the Marble Arch corner of the park, I could see the buses driving down what we called 'Rotten Row'. As I trotted up to the corner I would look across and time my turn just as a red double decker bus came into view. As I lined myself up, with the straight track in front of us, I would look over my shoulder on my right to pick the most likely bus to race. If Jo could have read my mind she would have herd me say, 'This one Jo, we can have him'. With Jo on my back and my blood starting to pump faster, I would hit the ignition button. Before Jo knew what was happening, we were off. I accelerated through my gears, up to top speed in seconds. Faster and faster, then faster again. From the corner of my eye I could see people on the bus turning their heads at the sight of this little horse tearing up the ground as I sped down the straight. With Jo, gripping me tight with her thighs, holding my reins evermore shorter, moving in time with my stride, her head down and my ears pinned back, I let it all go. As I hit top speed l kept one eye on the bus to my side. As I lengthened my gait, we would pull away from the bus and the race was ours. As we reached the quickly approaching corner at the end of the straight, I started to ease up and look across to the bus behind. As it caught up to me, the windows of the bus were filled with smiling faces all watching my glorious victory. As Jo sat back on my saddle and took deep breaths, I triumphantly rejoiced with, 'Yah! Well done Jo. We won, we won! – let's go home now.'

The officers were very careful to pair me up with lighter riders to look after my back. I was still quite a handful to ride and only the more experienced troopers were allowed to ride me. One such trooper was Lance Corporal Kevin Connor. I was Kevin's troop horse and together we participated in many duties together. I always tried to be a good guard horse for him. He treated me with respect, so, I in turn treated him with the same respect. The only thing I didn't like was when he touched my stifle. A man's stifle is his own. It was bad enough that they made me wear a crupper – a Leather strap which fitted around the base of my tail and buckled to the saddle, stopping the saddle sliding forward. The truth is that I was very ticklish. When I lashed out, it was to make them stop. I wasn't angry, I was just ticklish. A few times Kevin forgot about my sensitivity and I practically knee capped him. I was so sorry, I didn't mean to hurt him.

Kevin seemed to understand that my stroppiness was part of my character. I could be a real bugger in the stables. I would try and untie myself all the time. All Cavalry horses wear head collars at all times, which are tied to the wall with rope. My job was to untie the rope. Not my official job, but I did practice it a lot. By pulling on my rope or chewing on it, I could loosen my tether and my prize was to go for a wander. I would wander up and down the line of horses just being nosy. It broke up the boredom and it was fun.

I had a whole Olympic schedule of stable games that I would play. There was hay net volleyball, water bucket discus, yard brush javelin and my personal favourite, the nip the troopers bottom high jump or dash - depended on which way he was aiming in my stall. But seriously, standing facing the wall, tied to a silver ring, for hours on end was very hard. Yes, I would lock my legs and go for a sleep, but I always looked for games to play to relieve the boredom.

On guard duty I was a very different horse. I tried to be as professional as possible, solid, steady, but above all look after my rider. Sometimes the weight of the guard, his kit and my ceremonial kit would be too much for my back. Like I mentioned before, the pain would get the better of me and I would give my rider a rough ride; when a guard, in full Ceremonial kit, was perched on top of me the last thing he wanted was a bucking bronco for a horse.

Every year the Household Cavalry decamped to a small army camp in Norfolk. Bodney Camp was a breath of fresh air for us horses and no doubt for the soldiers as well. The camp was based in the heart of Norfolk, surrounded by acres of green grass and lots of trails for us to ride. Our time at the summer camp was not a holiday, but anything was better than being cooped up in Knightsbridge. As we were unloaded into the summer heat of Bodney Camp, some of the other horses went crazy, excited to be in the countryside. I, on the other hand, would just stand and take deep breaths, fill my lungs with the precious clean air, then go crazy.

The camp compound, when full of us Household Cavalry visitors, was like a mini village in the Norfolk countryside. The soldiers billeted in the old Nissan huts down by the gate. We horses were stabled in temporary stable lines, which stretched up the slope, taking up a large part of the camp. The Farriers had their own small building at the end of the stable lines. The Officers Mess was over on the left-hand side, the largest building on the camp. But the best thing about the layout of the camp was that just outside of the perimeter fence and gate was, as far as I could see, acres and acres of glorious fields to run through.

Although we were on summer camp our routine didn't change. Early morning mucking out, training for the troops and all the usual business to look after us horses. The same daily routine didn't have the same feeling when we were at camp. Everyone had a spring in their step. We horses were more alive and raring to go.

In each troop there were a certain number of new troopers who were learning the ways of the Cavalry. Each of the young lads had completed their riding training but you couldn't really call them riders. They had no real experience in the saddle. The summer camp in the wide-open countryside was the perfect place for them to hone their riding skills without being dangerous. Some of the new recruits had never seen a horse close up, never mind ridden one. I took my turn to be ridden by the less competent riders. I could feel their nervousness at riding me, their stiff riding posture and the heaviness of their hands on my reins. I always wanted to look after my rider, but sometimes my excitement would just be too much to contain, and they would get the ride of their life.

One such brave trooper, fresh from his time at the tank regiment, was trooper Warren Brown. As a treat for us horses, they would take us up to a beautiful beach on the North Norfolk coast. Holkham beach is a stunning stretch of golden sand which we were allowed to exercise on. We were dressed in a single blanket, no saddle, and the troopers rode in their t-shirts and shorts. It was a wonderful place. It was always a highlight of my year.

Warren was assigned to ride me on the beach that year. As we walked down through the trees and dunes onto the beach, I could feel he was up to something. Breaking through the tree line, looking out over the amazing view, I could feel the cool summer sea breeze on my face. I took a long deep breath. If you could have seen me, I was smiling from ear to ear. Our group of horses and riders walked two abreast, weaving through the sand dunes until we stepped onto the soft warm sand. What a great feeling. A soft, warm, almost fluffy feeling on my hooves, not like the cold, hard, stony terrain of the streets of London.

Warren and his friend trooper Phil Lythe chatted all the way from the car park to the beach, both laughing about something. As the troop reached the water line I started to paddle in the cool sea water, the officer in charge called us to line up for a Cavalry Charge. Warren had been told that I could be feisty and very quick. I could hear Warren talking to Phil and saying, "Come on let's do it". We lined up with the other blanketed horses with their sporty looking riders on their backs. I knew what to do. The order to 'Charge', was given and with Warren squeezing me tight, I hit the gas. The feeling was fantastic. The damp sand under me kicked up like a speed boats propeller spray. The ground was firm but light and I glided over it without it hurting my back. Warren and I were neck and neck with is friend Phil. We started to break free of the rushing pack. Warren kicked me on. "Come on Stirling, let's Go!" I could hear him shouting, so his friend could hear. I quickly realised that I was in a race.

Warren and Phil had hatched a plot to see who was the faster horse, me or Phil's horse, Phantom. The beach at Holkham is a few miles long and on the days that we horses were there people would come and watch us in the water and running along the beach. That day the spectators were going be treated to a very different sight – two horse, flat out, going hell for leather down the crowded beach, being ridden by two novice riders with no saddles to grip onto and no hope of controlling us at that speed. The officers went mad, shouting "Stop, Stop, That's an Order!", but Warren and Phil later claimed they didn't hear that order. Weaving passed shocked civilians,

Phantom and I had the bit between our teeth and weren't going to give up until there was a winner. Myself and Phantom were both known for being very quick, but today we both seemed to be running on rocket fuel as the competition got more serious. As I looked along the rapidly ending beach, with lines of civilians gathered at the end, I decided to break off the race before it was too late. I think Warren was sad about losing the race but glad to still be alive. I can still hear the officer screaming at Warren, when we joined the group further down the beach. When Phil rejoined the group and the officer had given him his dressing down, I heard Warren say to Phil quietly, "I told you they were quick. I'll get you next time."

I never forget Warren and what he said. At the end of our stay at Bodney, the officers held a cross-country race to put into practice all the skills that the riders should have learnt at the camp. When Warren was allocated his horse for the day's activity, he drew me. As we stood at the holding pen of the cross-country course, I could feel his anxiety subtly transmitting into my body, even his voice had a wobble in it. When I realised what we were going to be doing, I was so excited. I remembered Warren on the beach wanting to go fast and I thought 'If you really like to go fast, I'll show you what fast is.' I loved the cross-country course, it was always my chance to let it all go. When we were called up to the start line I started to almost jump up and down in anticipation. I don't think

Warren was quite as eager to go as I was. The bit in my mouth was being held back so tightly by Warren it started to hurt. Suddenly, it was our time to start. Warren released a little of the pressure on my bit and I bounded up to the line. Warren, trying to keep his balance on my saddle, was telling me to "Wow boy', 'Steady boy".

By the time I neared the front of the waiting horses and riders, I was like a coiled spring waiting for the off. Suddenly the signal was given, 'Go!'. Warren, still battling to point me in the right direction, wasn't quite ready for the kick when I hit my start button. My acceleration was instant and explosive. I was off. Running, eating up the ground, my back legs producing immense power, running faster and loving every second of it. Warren, on the other hand, didn't regain his riding position for some time. Arms flailing, with reins like washing lines, legs splayed like he was going down a helter-skelter and some very flowery language coming from his mouth. I don't think he was enjoying it as much as I was. As we reached the first jump I just took off, clearing the jump by miles. I didn't even brake my stride. As I landed I checked that Warren was still up top. His riding position had changed, he was now as flat to my body as he could get, legs tucked backwards and reins so short he was almost holding my bit. I couldn't hear what he was shouting because of the wind rushing past my ears was so loud. I might have been wrong, but I think he said go faster? Or was that slower? Oh well, I went with the first thought. The next jump was rapidly approaching. I could see the Jump Steward just standing with his mouth open watching us steaming towards his jump. I took the obstacle flat out, again. I was horizontal as I sailed over the jump. My front legs were stretched out as far as I could get them and my back legs tucked up neatly, I must have looked like Superman flying over the jump. Again, I checked if Warren had made it. Yes, he was still gripping on for dear life but he had stopped shouting by now. At every jump I checked that Warren was still clinging on. I'm sure by the time we reached the finish line, in record time, he thought he had been on the best roller coaster ride of his life. I said to myself 'Was that fast enough for you Warren?' No reply.....

Chapter 4

NORTHERN IRELAND

In the summer of 1997 I was loaded onto a trailer by a tearful Jo Darlington. I wasn't sure what was going on, but I didn't like seeing Jo cry. She gave me a kiss on my forehead and said "Goodbye, I love you".

The journey in the trailer was long, hot and tiring, by far the longest trip I had ever been on. From my standing position, I could just see a small slither of view through a high window above me. I watched as the colours of the landscapes changed as I passed through them. Along city streets full of red-faced people in cars. Along miles and miles of motorways, cutting swathes through fields of crops bursting with the yellow hues of harvest. Then over a deep blue seascape on a white ferry, with a green funnel, and on down narrow lanes edged with brown dry-stone walls, marking out fields of lush green grass, with signs written in a language I didn't recognise. Until finally the truck came to a stop.

As the back door of the truck opened standing in front of me was a familiar face, Lance Corporal Kevin Hodges. Kevin was part of the Riding Staff at Knightsbridge where I had just come from. Kevin had helped exercise me on a few occasions when Fraser was busy training other remounts. We got to know each other a little, he even knew my mother, Moonstone. It was good to see a friendly face waiting for me after my long journey.

I liked Kevin. Sometimes, I would just take a dislike to a person. If I didn't like you, you soon knew about it. I could be a real handful, if I wanted to. I would barge you over or push you out the way to make my feelings known. Kevin was a good guy who treated me with respect, so as I arrived on his Livery yard in Northern Ireland, I knew I would be looked after and be safe.

While Kevin was still part of the Household Cavalry he was sent to Northern Ireland to run an Equestrian Centre and Livery Stables in Ballykinler. Kevin was looking for a special horse to ride on the local equestrian circuit and he picked me from a list that the cavalry gave him of horses they could spare. I was included on the list because I was a bit too fiery and fast to be considered a safe guard horse, so I wasn't being used as much as I should have been. I like to think that Kevin picked me for my strength, stamina and of course my stunning good looks. A request for me to join Kevin was submitted and agreed by my commanding officer.

Over the previous year at Knightsbridge barracks, I had been ridden by many of the troops. Each Corporal of Horse who allocated me to a trooper for riding duties tried to limit the size of rider for me to carry. Nevertheless, I still had a bad back, which would make me very grumpy with the pain. The young troopers just thought I was a grumpy old horse, little did they know that it was the pain that I just couldn't bear, so I would try to be difficult to get out of riding duties. I'm not proud of it now, but I would spit at my riders as we were cantering in the park. If I didn't like the heavy rider on my back, I would get a whole mouthful of spit and just when we were transitioning from trot to canter, I would spit the contents of my mouth over my head right into the face of the trooper on my back. I think they thought I was just being vile, but actually, I was so angry at the pain from the weight on my painful back it was my way of expressing my discomfort. I'm sure the rider was horrified at getting a face full of spit, not my most endearing habit.

When Kevin Hodges inspected me as I walked off the transport from England, he moved his hand along my legs and back, noticing straight away how thin I was. I have always been a skinny horse, I've never been able to put on much weight, but Kevin could see I needed a rest from the heavy ceremonial kit and riders I was being asked to carry day to day on my duties. Kevin led me to a grass paddock by the yard. I could see the fields over his shoulder as he was inspecting me, I started to edge towards that side of the yard. As I reached the paddock gate, Kevin slipped off my head collar and opened the gate. By this time, I was dancing an Irish jig in anticipation of feeling the grass beneath my hooves. I nudged the gate out of Kevin's hand as he started to open it, and I was off. I ran to the far side of the field, forgetting all the aches and pains from the long journey, then dropped to my knees for a good old back scratch and dust bath.

For four months Kevin put me out to grass, building me up on a diet of lush Irish grass and a weight gaining supplement. It seemed to do the trick. I felt like a two-year-old again. While Kevin wasn't riding me, he had a local man look at my back problem. He reported to Kevin that I had a twisted lumber region around my loins. They decided that a probable reason for it was that I was broken in when I wasn't quite matured enough, but it was agreed that I was still young and it would, with rest, be able to rectify itself in time.

The land around Ballykinler was beautiful with rolling fields of grass, bisected by stone walls, as far as I could see. Kevin's Equestrian Centre was right near the sea, most days he would ride me down to the beach for a run along the sand. When the tide went out, the beach opened up to six miles of pure golden sand and we could run all the way to Newcastle beach. The first time Kevin took me out through the back gates of his fields and down to the dunes, it reminded me of the beach at Holkham. Just like Holkham in Norfolk, the beach was ironing board flat and looked amazing under the vast sky of the Northern Irish coast. As we made our way through the dunes at the edge of the sand, I could taste the salty air from the sea spray and all I wanted to do was go for a swim. Full of excitement at going for a dip, I took off with Kevin holding tight. In seconds, I hit top speed as I headed for the waves, taking Kevin by surprise. We raced, head on to the water's edge, Kevin gripping me tightly tried to slow me up as my hooves felt the cold water and splashed up onto my belly. I didn't take my foot of the accelerator and kept going full speed, further into the shallow water. Kevin at this point was holding onto my ears for his life. As the water reached my belly, I took a massive leap. Like a breaching dolphin, clearing the water before nose diving into the sea, I jumped head first into the water. I don't know when I lost Kevin but when I turned to look for him he was standing waste deep in the surf, soaking wet, with a look of wonder at what had just happened. A pod of seals, bobbing around in the surf, saw what had just happened and nodded their approval at my perfect '10' dive. Kevin would take me for a swim all the time, we loved nothing better than messing around in the surf having fun.

Another regular ride out with Kevin was to go to a local gallops to run with the a stable of race horses as they exercised and worked on their speed training. It was always an early morning ritual whatever the Irish weather threw at us. Kevin loved to give the local horses a real run for their money, he didn't need to ask me twice. I seemed to find an extra yard of speed when the racehorses would push me to my limit. I would lengthen my gate towards the middle of the gallops, really stretch out to eat up the ground and we would pull away leaving the locals gasping behind. A couple of times I heard Kevin say "Oh My God!" when I lengthened my stride and really went for it. Kevin was a really good rider and he could always get that bit extra out of me.

Once Kevin thought my back was strong enough we started to compete on the local show jumping circuit. We did about thirty events in all, while I was in Ireland with Kevin, we always came in the top five. The same could not be said for dressage competitions. I didn't like them very much. To try and calm me down enough for me to even enter the arena, Kevin would exercise me for an hour and a half before each round, getting rid of my urge to go fast, even when I walked. So, we mostly concentrated on show jumping events, even when I could go too crazy some times. At a competition on the Tyrella estate, I clean jumped a table top jump which more than surprised Kevin and the crowd. It got our picture in the paper though. I heard Kevin telling a friend that when you're sitting on me, you feel my energy bubbling underneath you and when its released, it's like sitting on a cannonball.

The only thing I didn't like about Northern Ireland was the storms that used to roll up from the Atlantic sea. The thunder was horrendous. One night, I got myself in such a state as the claps of thunder rolled around the countryside; Kevin thought it best to bring me into the stables to wait out the storm. All night the noise just got louder and louder and I was beside myself with fear. Kevin sat with me the whole night, trying to reassure me and calm me down. I was very glad of the company. I'll never forget that night, I hope to never experience a night like it again.

Chapter 5

BACK IN THE TROOPS

After two and a half years living the high life with Kevin Hodges in Northern Ireland, I came down to earth with a bang, as the tail gate of the trailer hit the concrete of the courtyard in Knightsbridge barracks. My time with Kevin had come to an end. Kevin and I where recalled to Knightsbridge to rejoin the ranks of the Life Guards and resume duties. It was a shock to look out of the trailer and see the same red brick building facing me across the yard. With every stride closer to the entrance to the stable, I felt myself physically deflating. In a flash, I felt all the old feelings of confinement, frustration, sadness came flooding back. I really didn't want to be back in the Knightsbridge, I wanted to be back on the beach at Ballykinler, running free along the beach, under the wide-open skies that I saw every day. Instead, I was back in my cramped stall, tethered to the wall, wondering when I would see daylight again. That was a hard time for me. I was very angry and I took it out on whatever or whoever I could. I started to live up to my reputation as a grumpy little man.

Knightsbridge barracks could hold up to 260 horses with 150 horses in the squadron and 50 in each troop. I found myself back in the Life Guards as one horse in a large machine. It was very hard to get used to the squadron's ways again. In Ireland, I had been looked after and ridden everyday by one man. I realised that I was a one man's horse. I was Kevin's horse. Being back in the troop meant I was groomed and ridden by a whole host of strangers. I didn't even know their names. I just felt like a machine, a horse shaped vehicle, left in the car pool until it was hired out by anyone, no matter what experience they had at driving a Ferrari. I fought to be an individual in the ranks. I would not be broken by the system and the circumstances. I was Stirling 7447, a very unique and important horse of the Life Guards squadron. With my personal pep talk ringing in my ears, I stretched up to my full height, head held high, my chest pumped full of air, my back straight and strong and I resolved to believe in my inner strength again.

My return from Northern Ireland saw me assigned to 3 Troop, the Life Guards, my very first troop where I started my military career. 3 Troop was just the same as I had left it, just different faces. When I had a chance, I untied my rope and went looking for my mother, Moonstone. I looked along the lines of stalls, checking each horse, before I was spotted by a guard. I didn't find her in her old stall or any of the other occupied boxes. I later found out that she had passed away in 1999, the year before I had returned to the troop.

My reputation as a 'fiery little man' had been noted by 3 Troops Corporal of horse. I was again deemed too unpredictable to be ridden by the regular troopers for ceremonial duties. I was assigned to a more accomplished rider called Lance Corporal Ricky Mountford. Ricky was a good balanced rider who seemed to understand my character. The first time Ricky rode me was on a Queens Escort rehearsal, one Ricky would never forget.

Escorting the Queens carriage is a great honour for us Life Guards. We take our parade duties very serious. The commanding officers ordered a rehearsal in Hyde Park to sharpen our abilities to protect the Queen's carriage in the event of an attack. We have two important scenarios for a situation with the carriage. The green scenario is when the carriage has been assaulted or the queen has been taken ill, but is still moving. The Red scenario is when the carriage has stopped and something drastic has happened. Two very serious events.

Ricky Mountford was assigned to ride me for the rehearsal. Ricky had been instructed to ride rear guard at the back of the escort. From where Ricky and myself were lined up, we could see right down the lines of horses and guards, to the carriage and beyond, right up to the leading group of the escort. What a sight. At the briefing for the rehearsal, Ricky and the other guards had been told to be on the lookout for a rogue group of protesters who were planning to disrupt the escort and attempt to compromise the Queens carriage. In practice, if the alarm is sounded for any attack on the Queens carriage, a Red Scenario, then all the horses must surround the carriage, interlocking themselves to protect the Queen inside.

Being part of a royal occasion was something I had done many times before. Although this was a rehearsal without the Queen, we took it very seriously. Ricky seemed quite relaxed and I was excited at what might be about to happen. It was great to be in the park and about to play a game. I'm not sure if Ricky had been warned about me but he was a good rider and I tried to make him look good. Suddenly a group of protesters appeared aiming for the carriage.

A Red scenario alarm was given, as we were taught, all the horses and riders quickly started to surrounded the carriage, interlocking their bodies to make a barrier between the protesters and the carriage. Ricky and myself were two hundred yards away from the carriage at the sound of the alarm. I felt the hard spike of Ricky's spur in my side and I took off towards the carriage. I knew what to do. I had to get to her Majesty as quick as I could to protect her. As usual, within seconds, I was doing one hundred miles an hour. I think Ricky was taken by surprise, he almost slid off the back of my saddle with the acceleration, as I responded to his poke.

At break neck speed, we were hurtling towards the interlocking horses. Some fifty yards from our rear guard position, Ricky finally found his saddle again. At one hundred and forty yards to the stationary carriage, Ricky gathered up my reins and started to pull. At one hundred yards to impact with the gathered escort, Ricky dropped his sword to use both hands to holt the speeding train. At eighty yards and closing fast, Ricky started to panic, I wasn't stopping. I felt a massive tug on my bit to the right and I veered off, away from the car crash that was about to happen. Ricky regathered my reins, only to look up and see I was now on a direct collision course with an under-10's football match. I didn't want to go that way, the carriage was over there, that's where we should be. So, I quickened my pace again, and swerved back to the direction of the carriage which was by now sixty yards away.

As I altered course, I saw a Helmet wizz by my ears. Suddenly, I felt a hand reach around and grab my bit in my mouth. With all his might Ricky pulled my bit, the pain startled me. I instantly put the brakes on, only to see Ricky flying over my head like a shiny rocket entering the earth's atmosphere. Ricky rolled down the road, over and over, until he came to a skidding stop, on his back. Lying on his back in front of the protective cordon around the carriage, Ricky slowly opened his eyes. As he came too, dazed and not sure what just happened, I walked up to him and nudged him with my nose and asked him, 'What you doing down there?' No reply...

Sitting in the Queens carriage watching all that had just happened was a Major General. Ricky was helped to his feet, as the General climbed from the carriage laughing.

He explained to Ricky, he had watched the whole thing, and the funniest part was when I went over and nudged Ricky on the floor as if to say 'Get Up Man'.

We arrived back at the barracks after the eventful rehearsal and Ricky dismounted to the sound of a few calls from his fellow guards. I heard some of the troopers saying, "That horse is mad". But straight away, Ricky defended me, replying, "No, that horse is Hilarious." Ricky was right, I wasn't mad. I just got a bit over excited about doing my duty.

The annual summer camp at Bodney Camp in Norfolk was an opportunity to blow the city air out of my body and have a bit of fun. At the end of each camp, the Household Cavalry held an Open Day for the local towns and villages. I loved those Open Days. I would get a chance to show off. The families who came to see us horses, would buy a bag or two of carrots at the gate and then walk the lines of temporary stabled horses. Some of the horses weren't very friendly to our guests. They would bite people. I wasn't like that. I loved it when the families would stop at my stall, feed me carrots and generally make a fuss of me. Standing at the door of my stall, with my neck as far into the aisle as possible, I would pull faces to make people stop and feed me.

The local families seemed to really enjoy meeting us horses and chatting to the troopers. With their bulging bags of carrots in their hands, the families would look for a friendly looking horse to feed. My face pulling trick worked every time and Dad's with their little daughters on their shoulders, held out their tiny hands, tightly gripping half a carrot. The dad would quietly reassure his daughter, "He won't bite", as I inched closer to the tasty carrot. Gently, I took the carrot into my mouth and to make them laugh, I would always use my lips to tickle them on the hand. It always made them jump. As the little girl pulled her hand away, I would hear her laugh and grab dads head tightly.

Next up, braver big brothers would step forward. As they looked up at me towering above them, they stood right in front of me and held their carrots high in the air, like they were holding a flag in the wind. As I slowly leant down and bit the tops off their carrots in their hands, I would see their eyes were tightly closed, just in case something happened. But when they realised I had taken a bite and all was still OK, the look of amazement in their eyes as they turned to their parents, was priceless. By the end of the day, I was always sure I had carrot poisoning, or had I just eaten too much?

Another big attraction on the open day is the main arena. Throughout the day different horses and riders showcase their skills at tent pegging, show jumping and other competitions. Ricky and I were asked to take part in an obstacle race just perfect for my skills. You needed to be fast and agile to win the race between teams of troopers.

The idea of the obstacle course was to show our speed, agility and the rider's horsemanship over a course of jumps, slalom poles and a few other tricks along the way. The first team to take it in relays and complete the short course were the winners. Ricky and myself were allocated the last leg for our team. By the time it came to Ricky and my turn, there was only three horses left standing on the course. The noise of the crowd screaming for their chosen team and the noise of the balloons popping as part of the obstacles, proved too much for some of the horses. As I looked around, all you could see was horses with young riders running in all directions, frightened by the noise and commotion. As Ricky popped the last of the balloons on poles in our lane, we only had one obstacle left, right in front of the commanding officer. The last obstacle was a balloon anchored to the ground which Ricky had to pop using his sword. I had completed the leg in super-fast time and Ricky was trying to slow me up to have a chance at popping the final balloon at the first attempt. Ricky took a look over his shoulder to see were the competition was. There were troopers lying all over the course. Riderless horses were disappearing off into the distance. Ricky realised it was just us holding centre stage. I slowed to a trot as we reached the final balloon in front of the commanding Officer. Ricky whispered to me, "Let's make it a big finish". As Ricky saluted the officer then drew his sword I came to a stand-still. I could hear the crowd cheering, the commentator on the tannoy announced our names to the clapping crowd. Ricky bent down and popped the final balloon. As Ricky rose to take the crowds applause, I decided that we weren't done yet. I reared up on my back legs to my full height, with Ricky still holding his sword in a triumphant gesture, I hopped back until I jumped onto the next lanes balloon. As the balloon popped, with me rearing up and Ricky with his sword heroically aloft, we looked like a conquering hero and his magnificent charger in a grand old painting. The crowd went wild. 'Now that was how to make a big finish', I thought to myself.

I loved the limelight. I loved to be the center of attention. I remember one such occasion when the Household Cavalry opened its Museum in Whitehall, Central London. The grand occasion was attended by the Queen and Prince Philip. The organisers of the event wanted to make a grand spectacle by parading a troop of camels alongside us horses, to celebrate the role camels had played in the history of the Household Cavalry. On paper it must have looked good. Two lines of animals parading as one in front of the Queen. A spectacle never seen in Whitehall before, the only trouble was, in reality horses and camels don't mix well together. In fact, when the organisers' ran a rehearsal for the event, all but one cavalry horse refused to go anywhere near the camels. That brave lone horse was me. I was the only horse that didn't turn tail and run at the sight of the camels. That meant, the stage was all mine. As the line of camels and I paraded past the Queen and Prince Philip, I was proud to represent the whole House Hold Cavalry. Secretly, I said to myself 'No one is upstaging me, especially a camel'.

I may have been one of the smallest horses in the Cavalry but I had one of the biggest attitudes in the Regiment. Over the years spent in the Life Guards Mounted Regiment I had been ridden by many troopers. Some of these brave souls had risen to the challenge I posed, others fell by the wayside. One trooper who met my challenge head on was a trooper from South Africa who joined the Household Cavalry to make a mark. Jacobus Viljeon was a real Knightsbridge Warrior. He was dedicated to being the best solider he could be. I think that's why we really got on. I always wanted to do my duty to the best of my ability.

Jacobus was a great Life Guard. He was one hundred percent dedicated to being the model Queens Life Guard. Jacobus would spend hours polishing and preparing his and my ceremonial kit for our duties together. A Life Guard's kit is his obsession. The troopers spent hours washing, cleaning, waxing, polishing and buffing their kit well into the early hours of the morning. The public have no idea the hours of work that goes into a guard and his horse standing in a box at Horse Guards Parade.

Guard Duty at Horse Guards Parade was not my favourite part of my job. It was hard for me but harder work for the busy Guard. On the morning of the Horse Guards duty I would be taken, with only a blanket on, to the indoor riding school for a run. My rider would exercise me for the day's events by giving me a good stretch out; for the next twenty-four hours we were going to be at Horse Guards Parade unable to leave the guard stable to exercise.

A guard detail is made up of ten troopers: Four Box Guards with horses and six foot Guards. All guards aimed to be assigned box 1 Guard position overlooking Whitehall. If the Queen was in residence at Buckingham Palace then the Guard was made up of ten Guards, a Regimental trumpeter, two non-commissioned officers, a Corporal Major and a Commanding Officer. To be chosen to guard a box, you had to be judged the best turned out on parade. Jacobus took this duty very serious and did everything he could to be the best turned out on the parade.

My first few months spent with Jacobus saw him put a lot of time and effort into getting my Ceremonial kit looking it's best. Every buckle, strap and inch of saddle was lovingly polished until it shone like new – good enough to win the Richmond Cup any day. When we were dressed and paraded for inspection, I felt proud to be Jacobus's mount. Standing to attention with Jacobus on my back, dressed in his spotless scarlet tunic, dazzlingly white britches and impossible shiny helmet with a sleek white plume to top it all – we looked every inch the model Life Guard and his Horse.

I must admit, dressed in my Ceremonial kit, I looked a real 'Dapper Dan'. I made my riders look good. I projected the perfect image of a war horse. Fast, agile, brave and dapper, everything a good Cavalryman's horse should be. I think because of this, I helped advance some troopers careers by getting them noticed. If a guard looked right and was good with his kit preparation, then he was picked as the box 1 Guard. If the inspecting officer was looking for a guard to send for an advanced training course, or better still promotion, the chances were that he would remember my rider as a perfect Guard candidate. In fact, that's exactly what happened. Jacobus and myself would be allocated the number one Guard box every duty. When his ability and dedication was noticed, Jacobus was picked to be part of the 'Blue Mafia', an instructor on the riding staff - Lance Corporal Jacobus Viljeon.

As an instructor, you could pick any horse from the ranks to use as your allocated horse. Jacobus chose me to ride and together we worked hard to hone our teamwork across all the disciplines of the Household Cavalry. Jacobus got to know me well and our friendship grew. There was nothing that we didn't excel at - show jumping, tent pegging or ceremonial duties. I still could surprise him now and then with my speed or fun and games, but Jacobus seemed to take it all in his stride.

One of the training games Jacobus played with the troops was a mixture of horse handball and basketball. The game would take place in the indoor school with two teams of riders and horses. Because I was smaller than the other horses, the riders thought they could muscle me out of the game. Well, Jacobus and I showed them.

The other team would try and barge me out the way, rough me up. They tried to push me into the corners but I would see a gap and before they could block me off, I would zip through them and be in on the basket. The boys on their bigger horses had no chance of stopping me. I was way too nimble on my feet, dodging and weaved my way through the crowd and scoring at will. I was just too fast for them. I was a real pocket rocket. I loved that game. I loved any game which was fast, physical and adrenaline packed.

Chapter 6

A STRIDE TOO FAR

In my life, as in any games I played, I always had my way of doing things. I didn't like to be told what to do. I think it was the Hungarian spirit in me that set me apart from the other Cavalry Blacks. I was born to run, to run fast, to express my personality, to feel free and never stop. I will always be grateful to my father for the genes that made me extraordinary.

Like many riders before him, Jacobus tried to control my blistering speed. When Jacobus and I rode out, he would always keep me on a short rein. When a less experienced rider exercised me he soon had to find a way of controlling my urge to run. Sometimes it didn't end well. I could be a real handful if you didn't know how to handle me. I never wanted to put my rider's life in danger, but if they weren't ready for me, then they had to look out. Unlike the riders, I was always in total control. My theory was 'I knew best'. That worked fine until one horrible day at the summer camp in Bodney when my speed finally got me into a situation that I couldn't control.

At the end of the Bodney Summer Camp, the officers always organised a cross-country race as a final excitement before we were all packed up and shipped back to Knightsbridge for another year. I knew the race was coming up. I'd been at enough of the summer camps to know the schedule. I was really looking forward to showing off my stuff. This was my last chance to show all the younger horses that I was still a force to be reckoned with, before being cooped up in Knightsbridge for another year.

I was allocated a young inexperienced rider for the race, which I didn't think would be a problem, as I was going to do my own thing anyway. Jacobus had spoken to the young rider and told him I was fast and to watch I didn't get too close to the jumps. The young rider nodded and readied me for the race. I could feel his nervousness in his hands as he brushed me. I think it was his first time on the course, and to be told you're just about to ride into the unknown on a cannonball, really ramped up the pressure.

Every year, the cross-country competition is a big event amongst the troops. Some of the riders really fancied themselves to win and the banter between the riders was always great to hear. My rider, on the other hand, seemed to be wishing for a very different race - a nice, easy, trot around the course, but I had other ideas. Jacobus, because he was an instructor, was not riding the course that year, he was assigned a jump marshal position on the course.

The riders and their mounts were called up to the starting line for the race. Each horse and rider would go at regular intervals under the stop watch. I was allocated to go quite early on. One by one the first horses shot off from the line. With each jolt of the next horses starting lurched forward, I felt my rider jump in his saddle. With each jolt of the next horses starting lunge, I got more excited to be off. At one point, I was jumping up and down on the spot. My rider tried to keep me stationary and at least pointing forward. Next it was our turn.

Let me tell you something. I was Nineteen years old, I was a 'fag paper' just over sixteen hands, I had a constant pain in my back from carrying the ceremonial kit almost daily, I was not happy to be going back to London, and, I hadn't had my treat that morning. I was ready to explode.

Go! As I pulled the trigger everything seemed to move into slow motion. My rear end dropped gathering muscle power as it deepened into a crouch. Like an Olympic power lifter, squat thrusting a new world record, I transferred all my pent-up frustration down from my haunches, through my back legs and down into the turf below my hooves. As the turf behind me was ripped from its roots, I threw my front legs as far out in front of myself as I could, clawing at the air, until they touched the ground yards from the start line. My head shot forward as my rump reached its maximum recoil as it readied itself to deliver the same power in quick succession. My front hooves hit the ground in front of me, I dug them in to the firm grass and clawed them under my body and out past my back legs eating up the ground. As I repeated the powerful motion, again and again, faster and faster, I almost felt sparks flying from my shoes as they hit the flinty ground in front on me. My take off and first few strides must have looked like a like a Farriers hammer hitting white hot steel with showers of sparks flying everywhere. I was off and flying.

As I hit second gear, I thought I should check if my rider survived the explosion. Rider in position? Check. Well sort of? Somehow, my rider had managed to beat the G-Forces of my take off but his positioning was way off. His weight had shot all the way forward in his saddle, his head seemed to be glued to one side of my neck, his hands holding the reins so tightly they were already cutting off his circulation, I thought to myself, 'Good Lad, Stay on'.

With a petrified rider on my back and the open course in front of me, I hit top speed, quickly moving in on the opening jump ahead. Each cross-country jump was designed specially to test us horses and our riders. The jumps were made of logs and tree trunks taken from the local estate, and boy they were solid. I streaked across the grassland, cutting a single furrow with my hooves in the turf, zeroing in on the first jump. My rider pulled frantically on my reins trying to slow me up, but the fuse had ignited the gunpowder and the cannonball was on its way. Yards from the Jump, I took off, sailing clear over the jump, not even braking a stride. As I landed, my rider shouted something which was too rude to repeat. Jump after jump passed and my blistering pace never relented.

As I rounded a marker and broke through a tree line, I sized up the next jump and accelerated again. The next jump was a double. I needed more speed. As I lined up the jump my take off foot slipped. Disaster. The lack of purchase on the ground resulted in me not having the right trajectory to clear the large solid jump rearing up in my face. I hit the front of the jump with a bang, my front legs crumpled underneath me. The momentum of my body pushed me right up against and into the tree trunk, like a railway carriage, out of control, going downhill, fast. I bounced my chest on the top of the trunk, I landed shoulder first with my legs caught underneath me, rolling over and over, I skidding to a halt. My rider had been ejected over my head at the first impact and lay yards from where I screeched to a halt. 'What just happened?' I ask myself. And what is that pain in my leg.

I lay heaped in a pile of legs, saddle and reins. Still breathing hard from the run. All of a sudden, I felt a warm surge of excruciating pain shooting up my front leg, it was agony. I groaned in pain, as I tried to catch my breath. I tried to get up by throwing my weight up and as I moved my leg in front of myself, the pain was horrendous. By this time, the jump marshal had ran over and pushed me down and back onto my side. I lay there gasping with panic not knowing what to do, and rolling in agony.

As I lay on the ground someway from the jump, I was surrounded by people leaning over me. Through the fog of confusion, I couldn't recognise anyone, just hazy figures holding me down and talking about what to do with me. I don't know how long I had laid there with the pain from my leg getting worse, when I was aware of a familiar hand on my neck and a soft-spoken South African voice telling me to lay there and don't get up. It was Jacobus. When I had gone down and the marshal realised how bad my leg was, he radioed for help. Jacobus heard the plea on the radio and raced over to see if he could help me.

A crowd grew around me and all I could hear was the word "Euthanasia". I didn't know what that meant but Jacobus became very animated and started pleading with the vet not to do it and give me a chance. The young lady vet examined me again and again and every time Jacobus and her would talk about possibilities, occasionally euthanasia again, then treatments. I didn't understand what was going on. It hurt.

After a lot of conversation, sometimes quite heated, the vet agreed to get me up on my feet. At last. I wanted to see my leg for myself. As the crowd lifted me and I stumbled painfully to my feet, I looked down and examined my leg. It didn't look right. Apart from the excruciating pain coming from my front leg, it just didn't respond to my movements. I thought to myself, 'This could be serious.'

Getting me back to Windsor was a painful journey. Jacobus was told that I was his responsibility and he was to look after me until the vet could do a full assessment back at the Regiment in Windsor. The scan showed that I had completely blown my tendon in my right front leg. A very serious injury for a horse. The usual course of action would be to put down the stricken patient, but Jacobus had convinced the vet to give me a chance and he would look after me.

Jacobus Viljeon saved my life. Out of the goodness of his heart he chose to stand up for me when I had no voice. I will always be grateful for his belief in me, that I could mentally and physically cope with such a devastating injury. He gave a broken old solider a chance. A true friend.

On my return to Windsor Barracks, Jacobus stabled me in the 'sick lines' part of the horses blocks. Every day, he diligently treated me under the guidance of the vet. I was there for two weeks, then gingerly loaded on to a truck and taken for a ride to a new home. What I didn't know then was that my injury had resulted in me being released from the Household Cavalry and I was signed over to be the property of my friend Jacobus. The year was 2008 and I had been a Cavalry Horse for Nineteen years, and now I was free, if not broken.

In order for Jacobus to keep me as his own civilian horse, he had to prove to the same vet that he could give me a safe and suitable home to be rehabilitated in. Jacobus moved me to a farm close to Windsor called White Place Farm. For eight long months I was stable bound, slowly coming to terms with my injury. Twice a day Jacobus and his wife Deborah treated my leg with cold water compresses, ice packs and gentle massage. The Cavalry vet came to see me once a week to check on my progress. The healing process took time but Jacobus and Deborah helped me through the worst of the pain. By week six, the vet was happy that I was well and truly on the mend. The biggest problem for my recovery was myself. I was such an electrified horse, keeping me calm was very difficult. I was so eager to be outside in the fields that some days I would bounce on the spot with energy. I was like having a lit stick of dynamite in a stable, it was only a matter of time before I was going to go off.

After such a pleasing report from the vet, Jacobus thought it best to let me out into a small walled garden next to my stable, before I injured myself further. With the stable feeling more and more like a prison, I was so glad to be out in the fresh air with room to move. There were many dark days while I waited for my leg to heal. It took all my resilience to keep thinking positive. All I wanted to do was be rid of the pain and be out running in the fields again.

With Jacobus and Deborah's love and hard work, I finally recovered from my injury. The first time I was let out into the fields of White Place Farm, I was so happy. To walk on the grass, to take the biggest breath of fresh air and to roll in my long-awaited dust bath was pure bliss. I owed my amazing recovery to Jacobus and Deborah, without them I would never have felt the rain in my face and the wind in my tail again.

Chapter 7

MY FOREVER HOME

After a long rehabilitation, Jacobus was at last able to ride me out on the paddocks of White Place Farm. My leg was getting stronger each day, but my days of jumping were definitely over. Jacobus was still a full-time Cavalry Instructor and most of his time was taken up with his military duties. Therefore, a decision for my future was now necessary.

To help with the care of his horses, Jacobus asked a young girl from the livery yard to aid him and earn a few extra pounds. Becky Olsen, was an eager young horse owner who offered to groom and care for other owners' horses to pay for her horse's livery. Jacobus asked Becky to help his wife to look after his other three horses while he concentrated on me.

Jacobus already owned three horses, which he looked after with his wife Deborah. There was, Tano, a retired racehorse, Sadie, a young Colt and Dipsy a large shire horse, who Jacobus and Deborah worked very hard to care for. With my arrival Jacobus and Deborah had their hands full.

As Becky busied herself with the other horses in the walled garden, Lorraine Olsen, Becky's mother, introduced herself to me and Jacobus proudly explained about my military career in the Life Guards and my re-homing. Lorraine listened intently, taking in every detail and our great friendship began. Lorraine, Becky's mother, was not a rider at the time but her two daughters kept their horses on the yard next to my walled garden. Lorraine, Becky and Loraine's youngest daughter, Emily, all loved horses - you could just tell. The girls had rescued an old mare called Missie from being abandoned and neglected, and that started a life-long passion for rescuing and rehabilitating unwanted horses. Missie was Becky's horse. A fine old lady who could be very grumpy at times. Darren was Emily's horse, he too was rescued in a bad state but he flourished under the care of the girls. And lastly there was Alfie. Alfie was Becky's younger horse. A fine herd of horses, all rescued by the family and given wonderful care and attention, a forever home.

Lorraine had never had a horse of her own before. She had spent hours helping her daughters look after their horses but always stopped short at looking for a horse for herself. While Emily and Becky took Darren and Alfie for regular hacks out, Lorraine would come and see me in the walled garden. We spent many an hour together, Lorraine

fussing over me and I lapped up the attention. She saw my good days and my bad days. It didn't seem to put Lorraine off, she was always caring towards me. Jacobus observed how Lorraine and myself had such a great connection in a short time. After a chat with his wife, Jacobus asked Lorraine if she would like to take me on as her own. When the offer from Jacobus was made to own me, Lorraine jumped at the chance of owning such a 'Wonderful Animal!' My reputation of being a 'grumpy old man' with a huge attitude and ego, didn't seem to phase Lorraine, she could see through my games to glimpse the real me.
Lorraine and Jacobus came to an arrangement and I joined Lorraine's daughters' horses at the main stables in the yard. Lorraine paid a pound for me, a token gesture, then I was ridden up to the main yard where Lorraine was standing. With Jacobus on my back and feeling the effects of my leg injury, for once, I wasn't trying to run full speed. As we approached Lorraine, with a beautiful smile on her face, Jacobus rode me leaning to one side. When Lorraine asked why he was riding me like that, Jacobus told her about my habit of spiting if I was angry at my rider. Lorraine looked horrified. I heard her say "Right. Ok. What am I taking on here?"

Lorraine as a young girl had been a good rider, but after a big fall she had lost all her confidence. As her daughters helped her on to my back for the first time, I could feel her nervousness. Slowly I moved forward with Lorraine gripping me tightly and we circled the yard. Lorraine sat upright, taking the chance that I liked her and wouldn't spit, then gradually relaxed into a more natural posture. I could see that I would have to look after Lorraine until she got her confidence back. Just before Lorraine dismounted there was a moment when we were moving together and she was relaxed and it felt right.

In the beginning Lorraine needed a lot of help from the girls. Lorraine needed to be shown how to ride better, to be taught how to groom properly and to work out the best way to keep my appetite satisfied. It was all a steep learning curve for her, but, Lorraine threw herself into her everyday tasks with all her heart and she soon showed me that she was able to look after me, I knew that everything was going to be alright.

Settling into my new family, Becky, Emily and Lorraine fussed around me to make me feel at home. Lorraine would groom me for hours. I had never shone so much. With Lorraine standing on a box with her brush in her hand, I felt the soft bristles on my itchy back. As Lorraine slowly stroked me with the brush, it was like a horses lullaby. It would send me instantly to sleep. We spent hours together, her grooming me, me snoozing, it was great.

Now please don't get me wrong, but there was a little hiccup in our new relationship, which Emily and Becky managed to sort out for me. Lorraine was so excited about having a horse of her own that things started to appear in my stable that, frankly, shouldn't have been there. I'm specifically referring to a small matter of a Diamonté head band. Excuse me, but I was an ex-solider, a proud member of the Queen's Life Guard with years of service protecting the Queen, but the day Lorraine went out and bought a Diamonté head band for my bridle, that was a dark day in our relationship. No distinguished old solider should ever be expected to wear such an affront to his manhood. I had suffered the well-meaning fancy potions, oils and powders that Lorraine had sourced from god knows where, to make me look shinny and new, but the new 'DISCO' brow band was just plain wrong.

I wore it once for Lorraine, as I didn't want to upset her and she was so pleased with herself. As she pulled the bridle, with the new band on it, over my ears and smoothed my fore lock to one side, making the sparkle even more prominent, I looked at the girls watching the grand unveiling of the new bling. Lorraine turned excitedly to see the reaction from her girls. As Lorraine spun around with the biggest smile on her face, I slowly leaned forward, looking past Lorraine's shoulder and GLARED at the dumb struck girls, as if to say, 'If either of you two laugh, I will kill you'. Thankfully, Becky and Emily stepped in and I never saw that thing again. They should have given it to Missie.

Missie was in her late twenties when I joined the Olsen family. She was quite a cantankerous old mare, but we respected each other and had a great friendship. I have never been good at sharing, but when it came to Missie my feelings ran deep. I could see that at her age things were getting very difficult for her and I always wanted to help. Missie was not a good sharer either, if any of the other horses tried to eat from her hay-net or feed bucket there would be hell to pay. I, on the other hand, had such a respect for her that I would allow her to be tethered up on the same ring and we would share my food or hay together. Lorraine and the girls were always amazed at our relationship. In fact, when Missie hurt herself on some barbed wire in the field, the only way Becky could get anywhere near her injuries was to tie her up next to me and I helped calm her down. Two grumpy old horses with mutual respect for each other.

My grumpiness would show itself in many ways, there was always a reason for my outburst. When I wanted my food, I would kick the door until someone gave me my feed bucket. If one of the girls smacked me for kicking the door, I would bite them. I wouldn't bite them because I was being wicked, I would bite them because I had asked nicely, for a horse, and they hadn't been polite and given me what I asked for. I was always misunderstood.

White Place Farm was a livery yard set in five hundred acres of land. Lorraine and I would ride out, exploring for hours. I was the first horse Lorraine had ridden for 20 years after her fall. As Lorraine's confidence grew bolder on my back, she would ask me to trot. Now, I love Lorraine, and I try to do whatever she asks of me, but when it comes to ridding I know best. Lorraine is not accomplished enough for me to go any faster than a walk. Its simple, she looks after me and I look after her. My job is to care for Lorraine and keeping her safe from harm. So, we walk.

When Lorraine and I ride out, I am always on the lookout for potential trouble. Although I have always loved to swim in the sea, when I'm with Lorraine I will not allow us to go in any water. Anything could happen to her. I absolutely refuse to go in the water. If she insists I just turn around and march all the way home to prove that I'm in charge. Once a Life Guard always a Life Guard, just a different Queen.

Lorraine's daughter Emily is an accomplished rider and when she took me out for a hack, that was a whole new game. If Emily doesn't ride me properly or give me the right signals - I don't respond. To ride me you need to give me respect and be on your game. After my injury I seemed to lose my zing but my mind is sharp and I never forget.

I didn't single out Emily for any exclusive treatment, Becky needed to be ready for my games as well. Becky would regularly school me to keep up my fitness. I think Becky thought she was schooling me, but in reality, I was schooling her. As she clipped on the long lunge rope, I would allow her to line me up, making a nice neat triangle to me, ready for me to walk around her in a circle. Every time I would have to remind her to give the horse, that your lunging, enough space by bucking at her to stand back. Although she didn't realise it, she was on the end of my rope and I was teaching her how to school a horse on a lunge rope.

Over the years, I have seen Becky and Emily blossom into accomplished horsewomen and wonderful young ladies. I've had the pleasure of watching Becky become a mother, with two beautiful girls. Emily, who was very young when I first met her, has grown up to be a credit to her Mother. I hope my mother, Moonstone, is looking down on me with the same pride that Lorraine has for her daughters.

In my own way, I think I've taught the girls a lot. Emily is a great rider thanks to my training. Becky is a very knowledgeable equine nutritionist; I'm very picky about what I eat. Becky has researched and developed a special diet for me to keep up my weight. Every morning I kick my stable door asking for my breakfast. My morning feed is a delicious bucket of slop. The bucket used to have carrots floating in it but my teeth aren't what they used to be and now it's just slop. Oooo! Slop. I dive into the bucket nose deep. I don't come up for air until the buckets licked clean. Next, I kick the door for a bucket of water to wash down the breakfast and clean my nose. To show my true appreciation, I try to give Lorraine a kiss, but for some reason she doesn't want a sloppy kiss first thing in the morning.

As part of my regular treatments, a local vet used to give me injections. I really objected to having it done. One day the vet, Robin, was alone in my field at Pump Lane Stables, fixing a fence post. I stood on the far side of the field and watched Robin walk unguarded to the broken post on the other side. As Robin started to fix the fence post, I slowly walked over to him without him noticing me. Suddenly, aware of my shadow crossing over him, Robin spun around. I bit him. I didn't bite him very hard, just enough to make my point. Robin yelped in pain and surprise. As I turned away to walk back to where I started from, I thought to myself. 'Try that for an Injection. Mate.'

My bond with Lorraine has grown into a spiritual connection that we both cherish very much. When Lorraine's mother became ill, I tried to offer her as much support and love as I could. Every journey back from seeing her mother in Norfolk would end with Lorraine coming to see me in my stable. I could tell she was heart-broken. Sad with the realisation that her mother was slowly ebbing away. As I offered her a strong shoulder to sob on, she talked about what she needed to say. I felt helpless to make things alright for her but I knew being a loving ear and warm shoulder for her to lean on was important. I would try and cheer her up by giving her, what she calls 'A little Love Nip' on her arm. That was my way of telling her, I loved her and all will be alright.

Lakeside Equestrian Centre, near Windsor is my home today and I love it here. Wide open fields to walk, warm stables to shelter in and lots of people to see and meet. One person who I met when Lorraine moved me to Lakeside was a groom called Smudge. Smudge, his real name is Davis Smith, is my groom. An ex-solider like me and he's my friend. In the morning he brings me my food, that's a very good way to be in my good books. Smudge will sneak me the odd carrot or two and he knows exactly were to tickle me to make me smile. We will both do anything for a Pear or a Custard Crème biscuit.

Can I let you into a secret? In my younger years I wouldn't let anyone touch my back end. As far as I was concerned that was my own private area and you die if you go near it. But just lately, I have allowed Smudge to tickle my back legs. Oooo! It's heaven. When Smudge comes into my stable, I look at my back end, Smudge get's the message and gives my leg a tickle. If you ever come to visit me and I look at my back leg PLEASE give an old solider a little scratch.

Lorraine has a lot of love for horses, slowly rescuing a herd of horses which live with us at Lakeside. With each desperate rescue, Lorraine's herd grows. In addition to Emilys horse, Darren, which was with us at White Place Farm, there is: PJ, Arthur, Monday, Tank, Queenie, Puzzle, Breeze, and Barnaby all living a charmed life at Lakeside. Sugar, Jigsaw, Daisy and Bobby have been successfully re-homed to new loving homes. I remember each horse arriving confused and scared as they were led off their rescue trucks, each one having a sad story to tell. I tried to be a strong father figure for them, explaining, "Don't worry, you're safe now, Lorraine Loves you. You'll see."

One of the horses Lorraine rescued is an ex-Kentucky Derby racehorse called PJ. He's my 'Old Mucker'. We love to be together, he follows me around the fields as we look for any mischief to be had and at night we 'talk' through the night, as our stables are always next to each-others.

At the beginning of 2019, I was very ill. Every day I had to be injected with antibiotics, you know how I feel about injections. Georgi Broom, the owner of Lakeside yard, helped Lorraine and her daughters to try and build me up to survive my illness. Georgi was a wonderful help, getting up in the middle of the night to give me whatever I needed. Luckily, it worked enough to see me through another year. I am now thirty-one years old and my back legs are very stiff and weak, but that doesn't stop me trying to escape my stable to wonder the yard unnoticed.

Despite the unflinching love and care Lorraine has always shown me, I struggle to put on weight. I've always been a skinny horse but at my age I need to keep the weight on to survive the cold winter months. I'm sure one Autumn Lorraine will have a very difficult decision to make about my future. I know she will make the right decisions when the time comes, but today is a good day.

My name is Stirling 7447, retired horse of the Household Cavalry - Queen's Life Guard and this has been my Life story.

My Friend, Stirling

By Lorraine Olsen

Today I said goodbye to my Stirling 7447, and my heart is broken. At the age of 31, with his mind as sharp as ever, but his old muscles and legs could no longer cope. It has been a hard year for the old man, and the virus that hit him at the beginning of the year, took its toll on his health. For me there will never be another horse like Stirling, and I feel privileged to have owned him for the last 11 years. Stirling was my friend, my confidant, my escape when the world around me got too much. He understood me. He looked after me. He knew what a bad rider I was, and when I rode him we never went out of walk. Sometimes a fast walk, but generally a comfortable walk. I was only ever the passenger, Stirling was always in control, keeping me safe. Even when I lunged him, it was always in walk. I secretly hoped today would never come, but was told it was the kindest act I could do for him on a sunny day in November. I am so so grateful to my daughters Becky and Emily Olsen who arranged everything, to Ben, Bjh Farrier, for being there giving his support, and especially to Georgi and Cerys Broom, who showed so much care and kindness to Stirling, my girls and myself. I would not have got through this without you. And Charlie Olsen, love you. My old boy Stirling is free of aches, pains and itches. He is in heaven with Alfie and Missie, and a large chunk of my heart. Stirling, THANK YOU for letting me love you. Will miss you so much.

ACKNOWLEDGEMENTS

Lorraine Olsen
Emily Olsen
Becky Olsen
Lt. Colonel Hywell Davis. Retired
Patricia Preston
Lance Corporal Richard Maxwell. Retired
Lance Corporal Fraser MacDonald. Retired
Corporal of Horse Joe Weller. Retired
Lance Corporal Kevin Connor. Retired
Lance Corporal Kevin Hodges. Retired
Lance Corporal Jacobus Viljeon. Retired
Lance Corporal Warren Brown. Retired
Lance Corporal Ricky Mountfeild. Retired
Debbie MacDonald
Jo Darlington
David 'Smudge' Smith
Yvonne Wyles
Georgi Broom
Jamie Broom
Bob Ramsey
Mandy Schutt
Kay Hack
Major I. W. Kelly. Retired

'Thank you for reading
my life story.
If you enjoyed my book,
please visit
www.asp-equine.com
to browse more amazing
equine life stories.'

- Stirling 7447

ASP EQUINE

www.asp-equine.com
email: alan@asp-equine.com
Contact: 07432708105

Printed in Great Britain
by Amazon

50036415R00057